**A** is for Arauz

 **B** is for Basquiat

  **C** is for Cezanne

 **D** is for Dalí

 **E** is for Evans

 **F** is for Freud

 **G** is for Gaudi

 **H** is for Hopper

 **I** is for Ipcar

  **J** is for Jones

 **K** is for Kahlo

 **L** is for Lewis

 **M** is for Matisse

 **N** is for Neshat

 **O** is for O'Keefe

 **P** is for Picasso

  **Q** is for Qi Baishi

R is for River

 **S** is for Sugiyama

 **T** is for Tommasi-Ferroni

 **U** is for Uzunov

V is for Varma

W is for Warhol

X is for Xcer

 **Y** is for Yacoubi

Z is for Zelmer

for Arauz

B is for Basquiat

C is for Cezanne

D is for Dalí

E is for Evans

F is for Freud

for Gaudi

H is for Hopper

I is for Ipcar

J is for Jones

K is for Kahlo

L is for Lewis

s for Matisse

N is for Neshat

O is for O'Keefe

P is for Picasso

Q is for Qi Baishi

R is for Rivera

or Sugiyama

T is for Tommasi-Ferroni

U is for Uzunov

V is for Varma

W is for Warhol

X is for Xceron

r Yacoubi

Z is for Zelmer

For Noah, Milo, Zen & Lotus

www.theenglishschoolhouse.com

ISBN: 978-0-9976860-0-5

K is for Kahlo

An Alphabet Book
of Notable Artists from Around the World

Written by Dr. Tamara Pizzoli
Pictures by Howell Edwards Creative

THE ENGLISH SCHOOL HOUSE

A is for Arauz

B is for Basquiat

C is for Cézanne

D is for **Dalí**

E is for Evans

F is for Freud

G is for Gaudí

H is for Hopper

I is for **Ipcar**

J is for Jones

K is for Kahlo

L is for Lewis

M is for Matisse

N is for Neshat

O is for O'Keefe

P is for Picasso

Q is for Qi Baishi

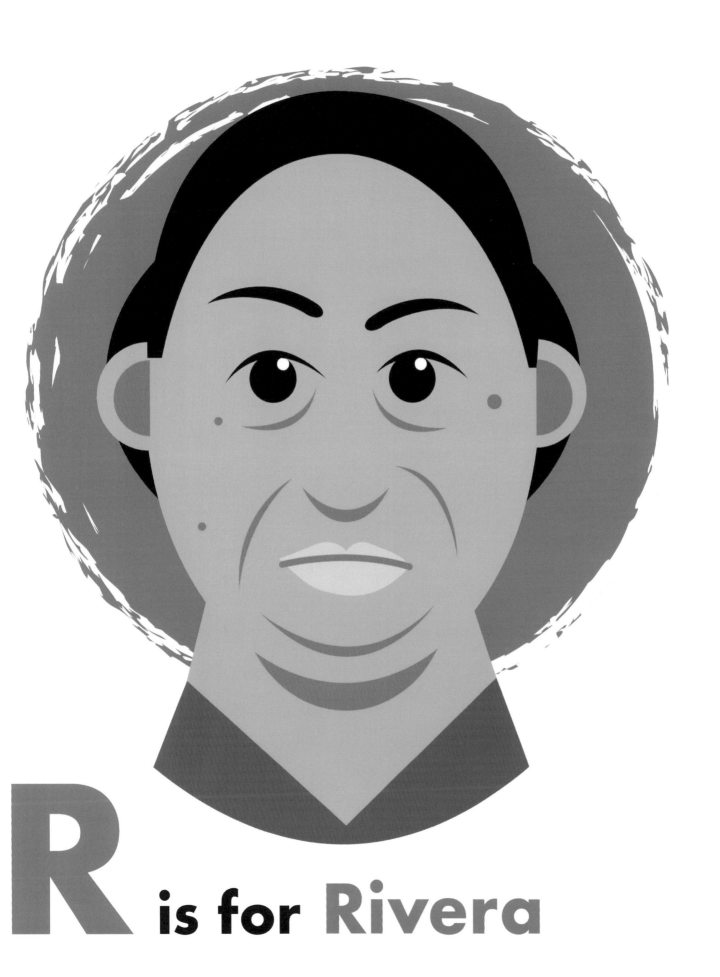

R is for Rivera

S is for **Sugiyama**

T **is for Tommasi-Ferroni**

U is for Uzunov

V is for Varma

W is for Warhol

X is for **Xceron**

Y is for Yacoubi

Z is for Zelmer

Arauz, Félix (1935-)
is an Ecuadorian painter. Staples of his work include the use of bright colors and subjects such as flowers and landscapes.

Basquiat, Jean-Michel (1960-1988)
was an American artist who initially gained opularity in NYC as one half of a graffiti duo. He later began creating works of art individually. One of his original paintings was sold at auction in 2017 for over $110,000,000.

Cézanne, Paul (1839-1906)
was a French painter. He is said to have influenced other great artists of the time, including Matisse and Picasso, and was known to be meticulous about the placement of each brush stroke.

Dalí, Salvador (1904-1989)
was a Spanish artist. Though he's best known for his surrealist paintings and eccentric character, Dali's artistic expression also included films, photography and sculpting.

Evans, Dulah Marie (1875-1951)
was an American modernist painter whose works reflected spiritual overtones. She also had experience as an illustrator and a commercial artist.

Freud, Lucian (1922-2011)
was a British painter who is recognized as one of the most prominent portraitists of the 20th century. He was the grandson of the famed psychoanalyst Sigmund Freud.

Gaudi, Antoni (1852-1926)
was a Spanish architect from Colonia. His most renowned work, Sagrada Familia, is the most visited monument in Spain.

Hopper, Edward (1882-1967)
was an American painter and printmaker who specialized in oil paintings , water colors and etchings.

Ipcar, Dahlov (1917-2017)
was an American author, illustrator and painter. Her most notable work primarily focused on colorfully depicted animals in a range of settings. During her life she wrote and illustrated many books for children and created sculptures as well.

Jones, Lois Mailou (1905-1998)
was an African-American painter whose artwork was heavily influenced by the continent of Africa and the Caribbean. Her work spanned seven decades and included illustrations, designs and paintings.

Kahlo, Frida (1907-1954)
was a Mexican painter whose self-portraits explored her personal narrative and cultural identity. Her work has been described as surrealist and feminist in nature.

Lewis, Mary Edmonia (1844-1907)
was an American sculptor of African and Native American descent who achieved great recognition as a prominent sculptor during her artistic career, which was spent mostly in Rome, Italy.

Matisse, Henri (1869-1954)
was a French artist who dabbled in artistic mediums such as printmaking and sculpting, but he is best known as a painter. He is recognized as one of the most influential artists of the 20th century.

Neshat, Shirin (1957-)
is an Iranian visual artist who is currently based in New York City. A noted filmmaker and photographer, Neshat's work has covered a wide range of subjects, including Islam, gender and ways of life.